T0194347

DAILY
DEVOTIONAL

DAILY
DEVOTIONAL

A Dealy Walk With God/
Declaring Life Changing Truths

120 Days to positive change

A k e a m   S i m m o n s

DAILY DEVOTIONAL
A Dealy Walk With God/ Declaring Life Changing Truths

KJV
Scripture quotations marked KJV are from the Holy Bible, King James
Version (Authorized Version). First published in 1611. Quoted from the KJV
Classic Reference Bible, Copyright © 1983 by The Zondervan Corporation.

iUniverse books may be ordered through booksellers or by contacting:

iUniverse
1663 Liberty Drive
Bloomington, IN 47403
www.iuniverse.com
1-800-Authors (1-800-288-4677)

ISBN: 978-1-4917-8914-8 (sc)
ISBN: 978-1-4917-8915-5 (e)

Print information available on the last page.

iUniverse rev. date: 02/02/2016

TO EVERYTHING THERE IS A SEASON,
AND A TIME TO EVERY PURPOSE UNDER THE HEAVEN

Ecclesiates 3:1

TO MY WIFE KIMBERLY

FOREWORD

Sometimes during our lives of chaos and confusion, we need a word of encouragement to help get us through the day. We should start our day off with a positive word from the scriptures to help us fight off the toxicities that we shall encounter.

This devotional was written to assist you during your daily fight to remain faithful and continue to grow spiritually in Him.

In order for us to reach higher and go further, we must believe in something that's greater than ourselves; something that is able to keep us during our times of struggle, but we cannot wait until we are in the storm to try and get ready, no, we must start our day with a Word from The Lord to prepare us before we leave our houses and face the trying world.

This devotional is designed to help you become better spiritually, emotionally, and physically in 120 days. Every day, start with an encouraging scripture, and a goal in mind that you shall achieve today-to make you stronger in The Lord.

Fight the good fight of faith, for others are counting on you to show them the way.

Be encouraged child of God!!!

DAY 1

1. I will lift up my eyes unto the hills, from where comes my help.

2. My help comes from the Lord, which made heaven and earth.

Psalm 121: 1-2

I will start this New Year by looking unto God to guide me through the valleys that lie ahead of me, and help me to appreciate the mountains that are sometimes before me. I purpose to not rely on my own strength and might, but look to The Lord to assist me through my valleys and over my mountains.

I'll not carry the baggage from last year into this year to foil my future.

This day, I shall walk in the newness of this new year, and expect change and fresh new moments that shall be best for me.

DAY 2

20. A man's belly shall be satisfied with the fruit of his mouth; and with the increase of his lips shall he be filled

21. Death and life are in the power of the tongue: and they that love it shall eat the fruit thereof.

Proverbs 18: 20-21

Today I will be careful of the words that I speak. I shall dispel negative speech, and declare positive things into my life. I will speak change and blessings into my life, and blessings into my family's life, as well as those that are connected to me.

I realize that my words bring to me whatever comes out of my mouth. I will speak it, and then expect what I have spoken to come to pass.

Today, my words shall move me into new situations and new fresh experiences; they shall open doors for me that were once closed in my face.

I will speak words that will close doors that are not good for me.

My words shall allowed my Heavenly Father to work on my behalf.

This day, I declare it and believe it. I speak it into the atmosphere, and expect that what I declare will come to me speedily and without hesitation.

DAY 3

As we have therefore opportunity, let us do good unto all men, especially unto them who are of the household of faith.

Galatians 6: 10

Today, I shall seek an opportunity to bless someone through my money, my time, and my talent.

I will bless someone and not expect anything in return, but God's favor for my obedience.

This day I am blessed, so I shall bless from that from which The Lord has given me.

I purpose today to sow into someone else's life; I will be a blessing to someone as God has instructed me.

DAY 4

Trust in the Lord with all of your heart: and lean not unto your own understanding

Proverbs 3: 5

Today, I shall gather the fortitude to trust God; even when I think that I know a better way, or when others are trying to convince me to walk another path. I shall trust God and not allow my common sense, or my five senses to get in my way.

I will trust The Lord to do what's best for me. My fate and destiny are in His hands………"I trust you Lord even when I don't understand what you are doing, or how you are going to work it out. I trust You!"

DAY 5

But seek you first the kingdom of God, and his righteousness; and all these things shall be added unto you.

Matthew 6: 33

Today, God is going to supply all of my needs. I shall have no lack; all will work out for my good.

I seek His Will in and for my life. My needs and my family's needs are met daily. He will lead me to the resources to meet my needs.

I refuse to worry about my needs because The Lord has already provided for me.

DAY 6

No weapon that is formed against you shall prosper; and every tongue that shall rise against you in judgment you shall condemn. This is the heritage of the servants of the Lord, and their righteousness is of me, says the Lord

Isaiah 54: 17

Today, my enemies will have no power over me. I will not be concerned about what they say about me, for God has already defeated them and hushed their months; that which they meant bad for me, The Lord turned it around and made it for my good.

Today, I'll not allow my enemies to discourage me, or hinder my progress. I will let God fight my battles, and I will right now shout the victory, for my enemies are already defeated.

DAY 7

Repent you therefore, and be converted, that your sins may be blotted out, when the times of refreshing shall come from the presence of the Lord

Acts 3: 19

Today, I will not let religion convict me with guilt. Jesus paid the price for my sins. I fully realize that I am saved now; not by what I do in religion, but by repentance and belief in the forgiving blood of Jesus that washed away all of my sins.

Today, I am going to walk in the joy of my salvation.

DAY 8

Let not your heart be troubled: you believe in God, believe also in me

John 14: 1

Today, I will turn all of my cares over to The Lord. I will cease to worry about anything, for I know that He has it all under control, and I am in His hands.

DAY 9

The earth is the Lord's, and the fullness thereof; the
world, and they that dwell there in.

Psalms 24: 1

Today, I accept God's plan for me, for I know that He has made a way for me. I am completely under His care and protection. All that I see belongs to Him; all that I touch belongs to Him, and all that I can ever imagine is already His. I praise Him today for affording me the privilege to enjoy the things that is already His that I might show and illustrate His goodness towards me.

DAY 10

And I saw a new heaven and a new earth: for the first heaven and the first earth were passed away, and there was no more sea.

Revelation 21: 1

Today, I will keep my priority straight and keep first things first. I will honor and love God and my family, and not worship the things that He has given me, realizing that someday soon I shall leave all of these earthly things here. God gave them to me to give me some comfort while I am upon the earth. I praise Him and not the things that He has given me. I cherish the breath that He has given me, and my loved ones that he put in my life for a season.

DAY 11

In the beginning God created the heaven and the earth.

Genesis 1: 1

Today, I will praise The Lord for all that He has made, for He created all things. This day, I shall praise Him for His creation and His creatures.

He made all things wonderful. Today, I walk in the awesomeness of His creativity, for I accept that it dwells in me. I expect to be creative today, as my heavenly Father is. Creative thoughts shall flood me, and cause me to create, even from that which is most common.

DAY 12

Brothers, if a man be overtaken in a fault, you which are spiritual, restore such an one in the spirit of meekness; considering yourself, lest you also be tempted.

Galatians 6: 1

Today, I will walk in forgiveness. I forgive all of those that have hurt me; all of those that walk away from me; all of those that deceived me; all of those deserted me, and all of those that lied on me. I forgive them.

Today, I realize that I too am but human, and have hurt some folks that now I too seek forgiveness.

I shall leave the past in the past and hope for a brighter better future where I have laid aside and buried all the pain of yesterday, and forgiven all that have come short with me in the past. I forgive them just as my Lord forgave me of my trespasses.

Today, I realize that un-forgiveness hurts me more that it does the people that I choose not to forgive, so today, I drink fully from the nectar of forgiveness. I forgive all that have wronged me.

DAY 13

Abide in me, and I in you, as the branch cannot bear fruit of itself, except it abide in the vine; no more can you, except you abide in me.

John 15: 4

Today, I will purpose to stay connected to the will and purpose of my Lord, to let my life be an example for others to see. I will remain connected to Him all this day, and show His favor upon my life, and the joy it is to worship and serve Him.

I am connected to Him. I belong to The Lord. I will refuse any and all things that will disconnect me from Him. He is the source of my strength.

The more I remain connected to Him, the stronger I get, the more that I am able to show His strength in weakness.

DAY 14

Now faith is the substance of things hoped for, the evidence of things not seen.

Hebrews 11: 1

Today, I shall live by faith and believe God that He will do everything that He promised to do. My faith shall create my own opportunities; my faith shall open doors for me.

Today, I will allow my faith to come alive and build new bridges for me to cross. All that I need to succeed is my faith. My faith today is moving and stirring the world to come my way; I shall watch my faith show that my heavenly Father walks and talks with me on a daily basis. With my faith, I'll go where I have never gone before, and leap upon places that were here-to-fore beyond my reach. By faith I shall achieve!

DAY 15

For verily I sayu unto you, that whosoever shall say unto this mountain, be you removed, and be you cast into the sea; and shall not doubt in his heart, but shall believe that those things which he says shall come to pass, he shall have whatsoever he says.

Mark 11: 23

Today, I shall speak to my situations, my circumstances, and my conditions; I speak life into things that here to fore have been dead.

Today, I speak a word of life and health over me and my family. I declare to that mountain of sickness be gone; I declare to that mountain of debt, be removed; I speak to those contrary winds that's blowing on me to cease right now. I command peace to flourish in my life, and confusion to be gone. I declare clarity of mind and clear thoughts of God's plans for my life.

Today is the beginning of a new fresh anointing upon my life right now.

DAY 16

And the Lord said unto Cain, where is Able your brother?
And he said, I know not: Am I my brother's keeper?

Genesis 4: 9

Today, I will be responsible for my fellow man; I will be more understanding, and be willing to lend a hand and assist someone else to be better.

Today, I will first seek to understand, even before I am understood, or when I am misunderstood.

Today, I shall allow my brother to vent upon me, though I be innocent of wrong doing. I shall forever remind myself that I am my brother's keeper, and be strong for him when he is weak and all of his strength is gone.

Today, I remind myself of brotherly love.

DAY 17

So when they continued asking him, he lefted up himself, and said unto them, He that is without sin among you, let him first cast a stone at her.

John 8: 7

Today, I won't be so religious until I deny my humanity, and I won't be so human until I deny my spiritual self.

Today, I refuse to let religion make me self righteous, and self absorbed.

Today, I walk in the full realization of who I am-frail and week, but at the very same time vibrant and strong. I embrace myself and others as being human and spiritual, capable of often times falling short of His glory.

DAY 18

Wisdom is the principal thing; therefore get wisdom; and with all your getting get understanding.

Proverbs 4: 7

Today, I will make the right choices, realizing that my choices have consequences. I will choose correctly and make godly choices.

Today, I will not make quick thoughtless decisions. I shall ask God to give me wisdom and understanding so that I will not suffer the fate of a fool.

DAY 19

9. Hide your face from my sins, and blot out all my iniquities.

10. Create in me a clean heart, O God; and renew a right spirit within me.

Psalms 51: 9-10

Today, I will run quickly to God and ask for forgiveness of my sins, and pray for my fellow man's sins.

Today, I shall plead the blood of Jesus for my sins to be washed away. I repent to God quickly while it is yet called today.

DAY 20

Let everything that has breath praise the Lord, Praise you the Lord.

Psalm 150: 6

Today, I will praise and thank The Lord for all of His wonderful acts in my life. I will sing praises to Him this day. He is the only true God that made heaven and earth

Today, I worship and praise Him; I allow others to see my praise of Him, for I am not ashamed of my relationship with him.

DAY 21

Brothers, I count not myself to have apprehended; but this one thing I do, forgetting those things which are behind, and reaching forth unto those things which are before.

Philippians 3: 13

Today, I am walking passed my past, and reaching for my future. My bright future!

Today, I won't allow my past to interfere with my present or my future. I am leaving the things behind me behind me. And, even-though I have not fully arrived at the place where God is taking me, I am still better than where I used to be.

Today, I embrace today and reach forth to my future.

DAY 22

I press toward the mark of the prize of the high calling of God in Christ Jesus.

Philippians 3: 14

Today, I have determined that nothing shall hinder me from my destiny. I shall thrive and move forward in-spite of any and all obstacles that might get in my way.

Today, I shall go over, through, or around my mountains. I am going forward, unquenched and un-wavered. I go forward my the power of God through Christ Jesus.

DAY 23

Jesus said unto him, If you can believe, all things are possible to him that believes.

Mark 9:23

Today, I believe in God, in me, and in my destiny. I believe that I can achieve whatever I set my mind to, or put my hands upon.

Today, I believe that good things shall come my way; I believe that I shall walk into the path that God destined for me.

Today, I believe that nothing is impossible for me. I believe I am blessed and highly favored or God.

DAY 24

After two days will he revive us: in the third day he will raise us up, and we shall live in his sight.

Hosea 6: 2

Today, I am revived and refreshed in the Lord. I can do all things beyond what I can even imagine.

My strength is renewed and refreshed. After being knocked down so many times, today, I am revived to live on better than before.

Today, I am made better.

DAY 25

Where no counsel is, the people fall: but in the multitude of counsellors there is safety.

Proverbs 11: 14

Today, I will listen to those that God has sent to counsel me. I shall seek Godly advice.

Today, I will talk less and listen more. I will train myself to listen even when I desire to speak. I will listen to The Lord and those that He has sent to speak to me.

DAY 26

For whosoever exalts himself shall be abased; and he
that humbles himself shall be exalted.

Luke 14: 11

Today, I will walk in humility, for I know that all that I have, God gave it to me; all that I know, God taught it to me, all that I have done, God allowed me to do, and all that I am going to do will depend upon The Lord.

Today, I humble myself before him in much gratitude and thanksgiving.

DAY 27

Every place that the sole of your foot shall tread upon, that have I given unto you, as I said unto Moses.

Joshua 1: 3

Today, I speak into the atmosphere and possess all that The Father has given me, and take back all that the devil stole from me.

Today, I walk into my blessings. It's already mine; I walk in the fullness of my son-ship, and all that I inherited through Christ Jesus. Today it is mine; I claim it and possess it right now.

DAY 28

17. And he bearing his cross went forth into a place called the place of a skull, which is called in the Hebrew Golgotha:

18. Where they crucified him, and two other with him, on either side one, and Jesus in the middle.

John 19: 17-18

Today, I rise up thanking The Lord for the price that He had to pay for my redemption. He paid the price that I could not pay.

Today, I openly confess my faithfulness to Him, and I worship Him for dying for my sins.

Today, I put first things first, my relationship to Christ Jesus. Whatever I am going through, I shall get through because Jesus gave me the victory a long time ago.

Today, I realize that the devil was defeated a long time ago, and now I inherit the spoils of victory-life, health, wealth, peace, goodness, etc...etc.

DAY 29

But he was wounded for our transgressions, he was bruised for our iniquities: the chastisement of our peace was upon him; and with his stripes we are healed.

Isaiah 53: 5

Today, I receive my healing, for The Lord purchased my healings. I declare I am healed from all manner of sickness and disease. I am healed in my mind from depression, dementia, and all sicknesses that disables the mind.

Today, I am healed from cancer of all kinds, tumors, viruses, and any kind of lethal disease. I am protected from the diseases that might float in the air or linger on any surface.

Today, I am healed and protected.

DAY 30

For God has not given us the spirit of fear; but of power, and of love, and of a sound mind.

2 Timothy 1: 7

Today, I will cast aside my fears, and walk in the courage of The Lord. I will not be afraid, even of failure, for I will continue with great effort until I am successful.

Today, I lay aside anything that causes my heart to fear, and I walk in love while I declare that my mind is sound.

Today, I will not fear because I have the power of the almighty resting inside of me and leading me.

DAY 31

Frt not yourself because of evildoers, neither be you
envious against the workers of iniquity.

Psalms 37: 1

Today, I will not allow evil men to disrupt me, nor will I be afraid of what they are doing, for I know that Jehovah is my protector and my provider.

Today, I will walk in the boldness of the Spirit of the al Lord.

Today, I refuse to be afraid and walk in fear, for I know that all of those that are evil doers shall soon be stopped.

DAY 32

Till I make your enemies your footstool.

Luke 20: 43

Today, I will not complain about my enemies, my haters, and those that might be jealous of me, for The Lord has made them my footstool to help me to rise up to where I am to be. Without ever knowing it, my enemies have made me better. They caused me to pray more, and to seek God daily.

Today, I am stronger and better because of my enemies, for they kept me on my knees and forced me to pray.

DAY 33

But they that wait upon the Lord shall renew their strength; they shall mount up with wings as eagles; they shall run, and not be weary; and they shall walk, and not faint.

Isaiah 40: 31

Today, I will wait on The lord to direct my path and lead me up to where He dwells. I will wait upon His strength to hold me when I need to be held. I will not be anxious to move; I will wait on Him to guide me and renew my sometimes failed strength.

Today, I wait on God to give me the fortitude to soar like an eagle, and to see great distances for what He has in store for me. I will wait on the Lord, and not get ahead of His plans for me.

DAY 34

This is my commandment, thatr you love one another, as I have loved you.

John 15: 12

Today, I will walk in love; I will love all men. I will love in-spite of, instead of because of. I will love as Jesus has loved me.

Today, I will look beyond my brother's faults and love him anyway, even while the pain that he has caused me is yet fresh. I will love the love of Jehovah. He first loved me while I was wretched and undone.

Today, I will show the Father's love through me.

Today, the phrase I love you shall rest upon my lips; I shall say I love you to my fellow man, and mean it.

Today, I shall allow love to direct me down paths that sometimes I don't want to go, but I will walk in love as Jesus did.

DAY 35

That if you shall confess with your mouth the Lord Jesus, and shall believe in your heart that God has raised him from the dead, you shall be saved.

Romans 10: 9

Today, I shall confess my salvation. I will not allow religion to make me stifle my confession.

Today, I believe that Jesus rose from the grave by the power of Jehovah.

Today, I confess that He is Lord of my life; I am saved because of my confession and my belief.

DAY 36

But my God shall supply all your need according to his
riches in glory by Christ Jesus.

Philippians 4: 19

Today, God has supplied all of my need according to His riches. Even when I cannot see my way, or how he's going to do it, God has supplied my need this day.

Today, I'll not worry about my need, for it is already met through Christ Jesus.

Today, I believe it and receive it; my need is filled in Jesus name.

DAY 37

And we know that all things work together for good to them that love God, to them who are the called according to his purpose.

Romans 8: 28

Today, I will praise God, for I know that everything that is going on in my life is working to my good. He is preparing me for something greater. The Lord planned the course and events in my life to make me stronger.

Today, I walk on with my head lifted high, for my Lord is turning my situations around, and making the bad things in my life good. Even when what I am going through does not feel good, I still praise Him because I know that it is working for my good.

DAY 38

There has no temptation taken you but such as is common to man; but God is faithful, who will not suffer you to be tempted above that you are able; but will with the temptation also make a way to escape, that you may be able to bear it.

1 Corinthians 10: 13

Today, I rise above my temptations; I won't allow myself to circum to my weaknesses, for The lord has already strengthen me to overcome them, and has already given me away to defeat all of my temptations.

Today, I declare my escape from the tempter and all the traps that he has diploid against me.

DAY 39

This then is the message which we have heard of himk, and declare unto you, that God is light, and in him iis no darkness at all.

1 John 1: 5

Today, I will no longer walk in darkness, but I will open my eyes to the many blessings that The Lord has bestowed upon me.

Today, I see how blessed I really am. I see new life pouring into my life, and so I seek to pour new life in my family and other's lives.

Today, I rebuke the darkness that try to cloud my way

Today, I will allow the light of God to shine forth through me so that others can see His goodness

Today, my eyes are opened, spiritual and natural, I see the light, and walk out of darkness

DAY 40

If my people, which are called by my name, shall humble themselves, and pray, and seek my face, and turn from their wicked ways; then will I hear from heaven, and will forgive their sin, and will heal their land.

2 Chronicles 7: 14

Today, I humbly asked for God's forgiveness for my many sins, and wrong doings. I turn, right now, from my wicked ways, and seek His face and His purpose for my life.

Today, I purpose a life of prayer; I pray for those that be in leadership for our country and our church-President and Pastors. I pray for the welfare and economy of our nation, and through prayer, lift up the down trodden and poor in spirit.

Today, I seek The Lord's face-His plan, His purpose, His message, His love, and His forgiveness towards us.

DAY 41

1. Man that is born of a woman is of a few days, and full of trouble.

2. He comes forth like a flower, and is cut down: he flees also as a shadow, and continues not.

3. And do you open your eyes upon such a one, and bring me into judgment with you?

4. Who can bring a clean thing out of an unclean? Not one.

5. Seeing his days are determined, the number of his months are with you, you have appointed his bounds that he cannot pass.

Job 14: 1-5

Today, I glorify God for the life that He has given me; I am thankful for Him allowing me to dwell upon His creation. My life is and always has been in His hands.

Today, I know that the boundaries of my life He has set, that none can shorten or extend my life, for it is in His hands. He has already determined a time for me to dwell upon His earth, so I give Him praise for every moment, and I thank Him for taking care of me during my sojourn upon His earth.

Today, I will walk in praise and thanks, for I know that my life, in comparison, is but short. I have no time to be jealous or envious of anyone; I have no time to be overly burden down my life's situations or conditions that is beyond my control.

Today, while I have the time upon The Lord's earth, I will change those things that I can, and not worry about those things that I can't, for it is all in His hands.

DAY 42

Verily, verily, I say unto you, if a man keeps my saying, he shall never see death.

John 8: 51

Today, I celebrate in Christ Jesus, for I know that through Him, I shall never truly see death. He will not allow the death of my wealth, or the death of my health. He affords healings for me. I live in the fullness of His grace and favor.

Today, I celebrate life in Christ Jesus, for He puts a hedge around me and all that is connected to me, that death cannot rob or steal what He has blessed me with.

DAY 43

1. O give thanks unto the Lord; for he is good: for his mercy endures forever.

2. O give thanks unto the God of gods: for his mercy endures forever.

3. O give thanks to the Lord of lords: for his mercy endures forever.

Psalm136: 1-3

Today, I thank God for His mercy, for having mercy upon me. He forgave me for my sins, and forgave me for denying Him through the life I lived. Even now, in this present hour, when I fall short of His will, His mercy pleads my case, and affords me new mercies every day.

Today, I praise Him for His mercy has kept me. I should have been cut off, but His mercy wouldn't let the spoiler slay me in my sins.

Today, I rejoice because His mercy endures forever.

DAY 44

If you shall ask anything in my name, I will do it.

John 14: 14

Today, I ask The Lord to bless me to walk in daily new blessings; I ask this because He promised that if I ask Him for anything, He would do it for me.

Today, I am expecting to receive His favor to give me a mind that is filled with holiness so that I will not ask for vain things to receive upon my lust.

Today, I ask for wisdom, to make right and good decisions. I ask Him to bless me so that I can be a blessing to someone else, and I ask Him for strength so that I might assist those that are in need of my help.

DAY 45

For this we say unto you by the word of the Lord, that we which are alive and remain unto the coming o0f the Lord shall not prevent them which are asleep.

1 Thessalonians 4: 15

Today, I shall release all of the pain that I have carried in my bosom for the lost of my loved ones, for I know that The lord shall raise them up again. I walk in the joy of knowing that they are not dead, but asleep until Jesus comes back.

Today, I wipe my tears and allow my heart to heal, for my loved ones are in the bosom and rest of The lord. I worship him, for I know that one day I too shall rest in Him until He comes back to raise us up.

DAY 46

Let not your heart be troubled; you believe in God, believe also in me.

John 14: 1

Today, I release all of the things that I have been worrying about, and I fully turn them over to The Lord. My heart is fixed and my mind is made up. I will no longer worry about anything, for I believe In The Lord, that He has the power to change and control my situation.

Today, my heart is at peace, for my redeemer lives. I believe in His power to rescue me right now.

DAY 47

Verily, verily, I say unto you, Except a man be born again, he cannot see the Kingdom of God.

John 3: 3

This day, I will praise God all day for the newness of life that He gave me. In-spite of my faults, my failures, and my sins, He saved me.

Today I walk in the fullness of my new person. I have been born again, and given the chance by Him to start a new, afresh again.

Today, I will rejoice in the realization that He washed me and made me new in Him. Today, I'll try my best to spread my joy around to others.

DAY 48

Put on the whole armor of God, that you may be able to stand against the wiles of the devil.

Ephesians6: 11

Today, I choose to be dressed in the Lord-spiritually and emotionally. I shall not let the devil defeat me in my family, on my job, in my body, or even at my church.

Today, I have chosen to dress myself with the joy of the Lord, and to fight the physical fight with a spiritual weapon. I will not let the devil rule me today. I will pray much, smile often, and speak softly with kind and gentle words.

Today, I shall bath myself and those that will allow me, in the spirit of the Lord, for I know that the devil is already defeated, and I walk in the victory; I claim it and proclaim it right now in Jesus name.

DAY 49

And the Lord said unto Cain, where is Abel your brother?
And he said, I know not: Am I my brother's keeper?

Genesis 4: 9

Today, I shall take note of those that I shall meet t, and those that are constantly around me, for I know that I am responsible for my fellow man. I will do all that I can to help them to walk in the light of the Lord.

Today, I shall endeavor to be one that they can look at and see the hand of God on my life.

Today, I will pray mightily for my brothers and sisters. I will lift them up to the Lord. Where they are weak, I shall lend them my strength, and when they fall, I shall be quick to pick them up.

Today, I shall endeavor to understand, even before I am understood.

DAY 50

But lift you up your rod, and stretch out your hand over
the sea, and divide it: and the children of Israel shall go
on dry ground through the midst of the sea.

Exodus 14: 16

Today, I know that I have all that I need to overcome any adversary that I might face, or anybody that might come up against me, for the Lord of host is on my side.

Today, I have all that I need, and I don't need that for which I don't have right now. I will use what the Lord has already given me.

Today, I will stretch forth my hands toward heaven, and receive the blessings that he has already given unto me. My mouth shall bless him and praise him for already giving me a way out of my conditions and situations.

Today, I bless His holy name for all that He has done and is yet doing.

DAY 51

Now the Lord had said unto Abram, Get you out of your country, and from your kindred, and from your father's house; unto a land that I will show you.

Genesis 12: 1

Today, I release all that have stood in my way, and forgive all that have walked away from me. I determined to forge ahead and leave all that hinder me from being and becoming my best and receiving God's best for me.

Today, I come out from amongst those that are not good for me, and those that do not wish me well. I pursue those that shall assist me in becoming better and walking into that for which God has designed just for me.

Today, I have chosen to leave behind haters, enviers, and idlers. I choose to move higher and become better; to reach further and desire more of God's best in my life.

DAY 52

Make a joyful noise unto the Lord, all you lands,

Serve the Lord with gladness: come before his presence with singing.

Psalms 100: 1-2

Today, I worship Him; I make joyful noises unto Him. I gather myself with other believers today to worship Him.

Today, I honor Him with my body, soul, and spirit. I lift my hands and raise my voice in total praise unto Him, for today is a day of worship unto Him.

I sing a song of victory, for He has extended my boarders and increased my increase.

Today, I will join others in praising Him, for He is worthy to be praised.

Hallelujah unto Him.....I worship Him on this day that has been set aside for worship.

DAY 53

Bring you all tithes into the storehouse, that there may be meat in my house, and prove me now herewith, says the lord of hosts, if I will not open you the windows of heaven, and pour you out a blessing, that there shall not be room enough to receive it.

Malachi 3: 10

Today, I decide to give Him the tenth of what He has blessed me with; all that I have belongs to Him, but He only desires ten percent of my earnings. Ten percent belongs to Him.

Today I worship Him with my giving back unto Him ten percent of what He has given unto me.

And, I purpose that even after the tenth of my earnings, I shall seek to give an offering. The tenth belongs to Him; the offerings belongs to me; I sow it from what He left me after the tenth.

Today, I choose to walk in the blessings of tithing, and I look for Him to open a window in heaven and pour me out blessings right now.

DAY 54

And I will make of you a great nation; and I will bless you, and make your name great; and you shall be a blessing.

Genesis 12: 2

Today, I shall set out to be a blessing to others, for I know that God has blessed me so that I can be a blessing to others. I receive my blessings to share with others that are sometimes less fortunate than me. He poured into me so that I can pour into someone else.

Today, I seek opportunities to be a blessing to someone else. I will share what my God has blessed me with.

Today, I walk in the blessings of giving. I am a giver; I am blessed to bless, for I am the blessed of the lord

Today, I thank Him right now in advance for the blessings that he shall pour into my life.

DAY 55

And now abides faith, hope, and love, these three; but the greatest of these is love.

1 Corinthians 13: 13

Today, I choose to walk in love, not a secular love, but the love of God; a kind of love that love in-spite of, not because of. I love all because God first loved me.

Today, I will bless because of love; I will forgive those that have wronged me because of love.

I love because the love of God showers down upon me. Love won't allow me to be defeated by strife, or arguing, or bickering, or jealousy; no, love gives me the victory because love gives me hope to see through hopelessness.

Today, love will help me to rebuild some broken relationships, and restore that which the devil tried to destroy. I can love because the love of God rests upon me.

DAY 56

When I was a child, I spoke as a child; I understood as a child, I thought as a child: but when I became a man, I put away childish things.

1 Corinthians 13: 11

Today, I put away my childish nature that has stood between me and my blessings. Those that I have been angry with, and those that I have refuse to speak to because they have abused me or misused me, I denounce my negative actions and push it aside.

Today, I will not allow myself to walk in strife as a child, but I will walk in the complete maturity of the spirit of God. I refuse to be angry at someone because they are angry with me.

Today, I will put away my childish behavior, knowing that God watches my attitude towards others.

DAY 57

And Caleb stilled the people before Moses, and said, Let us go up at once, and possess it; for we are well able to overcome it.

Numbers 13: 30

Today, I shall be an encourager; I will encourage those that have lost their way, and encourage those that have been working in the Gospel, and have become tired and weary.

Today, I will encourage those whose blessing seems to be slow coming. I will encourage my co-laborers to wait on the Lord.

Today, I will encourage them to know that whatever God has promised, He is well able to perform, and He will do what He said that He will do.

I am an encourager; I give hope to those that are ready to give up; I calm down those that are in upheaval.

Today, I will encourage because I choose to be an encourager in-spite of whatever I am presently going through. I will encourage others and encourage myself.

DAY 58

Now therefore give me this mountain, where of the Lord spoke in that day; for you heard in that day how the Anakims were there, and that the cities were great and fenced: if so be the Lord will be with me, then I shall be able to drive them out, as the Lord said.

Joshua 14: 12

Today, I am believing God and all of His promises. I claim the mountain; the mountain of financial freedom; I claim the mountain of good health in my life; I claim the mountain of peace.

Today, I want the mountain that God promised. I am no longer bound by my employment, or by my circumstances, or sickness, or debt.

Today, I choose the mountain of deliverance; deliverance from all that have held me back. I say unto The Lord, Give me this mountain that I am asking for today.

DAY 59

For God has not given us the spirit of fear; but of power, and of love, and of a sound mind.

2 Timothy 1: 7

Today, I will not let fear rule me. I will not operate out of fear. I will walk boldly in the Lord, and in the power of His might. Although I might confront adversity, I will not fear, for I know that the Lord is still in control of my life.

Today, I will walk in God's power; God's love, and allow Him to give me a sound mind that stays on Him.

Today, I will not be controlled by fear. I will push aside my fear and trust The lord who's the captain of my life.

I am not fearful, for fear is not of God; I cast out fear right now.

DAY 60

Now faith is the substance of things hoped for; the evidence of things not seen.

Hebrews 11: 1

Today, I choose to walk by faith and trust in the Word of God. I believe that today is a new beginning for me. My faith shall open new doors for me, and attract fresh opportunities for me and good benefits.

Today, I shall operate by faith, and not by what I see, or how I feel. My faith shall cease the tongues of my enemies, and put them to flight.

Today. I have a new beginning and a fresh start, for my faith has cleared the way for me.

Today, I will believe the impossible, see the invisible, and do the things that I have only imagined.

I am walking by faith...I am walking by faith, and trusting completely in His Word.

Today, my faith has created new doors for me, and close negative doors.

DAY 61

But We have this treasure in earthen vessels, that the excellency of the power may be of God, and not of us.

2 Corinthians 4: 7

Today, I accept the best of me is inside of me. I will stop dwelling so much on the outside of me and focus on releasing the giant that rests inside of me.

Today, I will endeavor to see things that I have failed to see before, that I might conquer those things that have been hindering me.

Today, I am the giant that God intended me to me. I am the giant that rescues others; I am the giant that can see what God is doing; I am the giant that look further down the road and realize what's best for me.

DAY 62

We are troubled on every side, yet not distressed; we are perplexed, but not in despair;

Persecuted, but not forsaken; cast down, but not destroyed.

2 Corinthians 4: 8-9

Today, I know that everything that has happened to me helped mode me and made me stronger; everything that I am going through right now, is designed by God to propel me to higher level in Him

Today, I realize that the doors that God allowed to be closed to me, was only because He has opened other doors for me, and is, even now, opening new doors and new opportunities for me.

Today, I realize that all of my troubles and all of my pain, and all that I have gone through was and is God's pruning ground for me.

Today, instead of complaining about what is happening in my life, and complaining about what I am going through right now, I shall lift up my hands to heaven and give Him glory for loving me enough to send some things, that sometimes don't feel good, to help me become stronger and better, so that I can see and appreciate my destiny.

DAY 63

This then is the message which we have heard of him, and declare unto you, that God is light and in him is no darkness at all.

1 John 1: 5

Today, I purpose to walk in the light of The lord, that I might see His goodness and mercy upon my life. I will walk in the light of forgiveness and love.

Today, I will let God's light shine in my life to cast away all the darkness that has overshadowed me-even the darkness that I've held on to; I relinquish it, and walk in the light of God.

DAY 64

And I saw a new heaven and a new earth: for the first heaven and the first earth were passed away; and there was no more sea.

Revelation 21: 1

Today, I rejoice in knowing that God has reserved a place for me in His new kingdom. I give Him praise today for the new heaven and earth that He has created for me.

Today, I praise Him for getting me ready for that great city in heaven where He will turn all of my tears and sorrows into joy. I praise Him for it right now.

DAY 65

The Lord is my shepherd; I shall not want.

He makes me to lie down in green pastures: he leads me beside the still waters.

Psalm 23: 1-2

Today, I will praise the Lord, for He has provided me all of my needs, and today He is going to lead me in the directions that I need to go.

Today, my spirit shall be quiet, I will not be upset by the things around me, and by things out of my control.

Today, The Lord has restored peace and good will in my life, and I shall share it with others. My face shall wear a smile and my voice shall entertain laughter.

DAY 66

And the Lord said unto Gideon, By the three hundred men that lapped will I save you, and deliver the Midianites into your hand; and let all the other people go every man unto his place.

Judges 7: 7

Today, I will not fear, though I might be outnumbered and have to stand by myself, I will trust God. I shall accept the victory, for God is on my side.

DAY 67

What shall we then say to these things? If God be for us who can be against us?

Romans 8: 31

Today, God is with me, so it does not matter who is against me. God and I, are the majority.

Today, I shall not fail; I shall keep my eyes on God.

DAY 68

And we know that all things work together for good to them that love God, to them who are the called according to his purpose.

Today, whatever happens in my life today, is going to work in my good, to my best interest. Whatever is meant to be bad for me, God is going to turn it around, and make it for my good.

Today, I will walk in God's purpose for my life. He shall make His way plain unto me this day. Everything is working to my good.

DAY 69

Wherefore comfort one another with these words.

1 Thessalonians 4: 18

Today, I shall purpose to give words of comfort to all that I meet. My words shall edify and exalt others to comfort. I will ease the broken hearted, and put a smile on the down trodden.

DAY 70

Therefore said he unto them, The harvest truly is great, but the laborers are few: pray you therefore the lOrd of the harvest, that he would send forth laborers into his harvest.

Luke 10: 2

Today, I will go about my day being a good representative of Him, for I am one of His laborers. I will walk so that others can see The Lord's hand upon my life.

Today, I will introduce others to Him, and try my best to show the benefits of living for God. I will constantly be aware of my actions and my words.

Today, I will be a good laborer for God.

DAY 71

Many a time have they afflicted me from my youth: yet they have not prevailed against me.

Psalm 129: 2

Today, even though I might be confronted with adversaries, I shall not allow myself to be dismayed, for The Lord is on my side.

Today, God has already delivered me from those that mean me no good, and wish me harm. He has prevailed for me against their traps that they have set for me. He has stopped their lying tongue on me.

Today, I will praise Him for prevailing against my enenies.

DAY 72

I will lift up my eyes unto the hills, from where comes my help.

Psalm 121: 1

Today, I will keep my head lifted towards heaven, for I know that that is where all of my help comes from. I will keep looking up and claiming the victory today. All of my help comes from the Lord.

Today, I expect God to send angels to assist me so that I shall not fail. God still sits high and reigns upon His throne; all the powers that be, are subject unto Him. I shall not be moved.

DAY 73

For you have delivered my soul from death, my eyes from tears, and my feet from falling.

I will walk before the Lord in the land of the living.

Psalm 116: 8-9

Today, is a day of praise, for He has kept me through all the dangers that I have walked through. He refused my enemies victory over me.

Today, is the day of The Lord; I will show others that he still rules on earth and in the lives of men.

DAY 74

You have loved righteousness, and hated iniquity; therefore God, even your God, has anointed you with the oil of gladness above your fellows.

Hebrews 1: 9

Today, I will start my day, and walk all through this day in gladness, for The Lord has anointed me with gladness.

Today, is a good day. I am happy to be alive. I will not let anyone spoil this day, or bring unhappiness to me. I will rejoice and be glad. God has anointed me with gladness.

DAY 75

Wherefore, my beloved brothers, let every man be sweft to hear, slow to speak, slow to wrath.

James 1:19

Today, I will strive to be a good listener, and be very careful when I speak-not to say the wrong things. My mouth shall be closed, but my ears shall be opened to hear.

Today, I am a good listener. I will not judge those that God has led to confide in me. I shall listen and pray, and listen even more. I pray today that God gives me the patience to listen, and the strength to hold my tongue.

DAY 76

You will keep him in perfect peace, whose mind is stayed on you because he trusts in you.

Isaiah 26: 3

Today, I will dwell in perfect peace; I dispel the storms that may occur in my life today. I will walk in the peace of the Lord's Holy Spirit.

Today, I shall share my holy peace with others, and help them through their storms.

Today, I will keep my mind on The Lord, and keep His words in my bosom that I will not fear.

DAY 77

Your word is a lamp unto my feet, and a light unto my path.

Psalm 119: 105

Today, God is going to guide me down the path that is best for me. He shall give me complete understanding and discernment of which way I am to go.

Today, The lord is going to order my steps, that I might walk into my blessings. My feet are the blessed feet that walk in the light of God.

DAY 78

And Pharaoh said unto Joseph, See I have set you over all the land of Egypt.

Genesis 41: 41

Today, I will shout and praise His holy name, for He is making even my enemies to bless me. I am blessed of the lord. Those that fight me, shall now assist me and help me to move up to higher ground.

DAY 79

And Jabez called on the God of Israel, saying, Oh that you would bless me indeed, and enlarge my coast, and that your hand might be with me, and that you would keep me from evil, that it may not grieve me! And God granted him that which he requested.

1 Chronicles 4: 10

Today, The Lord shall expand my boarders, that I might be able to reach and bless others for Him; God's hand shall be with me, that I might stand firm on His word to show others the way, and fight in His strength.

Today, God shall keep me from evil, so that I am not grieved or disabled by any evil. Today I shall be strong in The Lord.

Today, The Lord is granting my requests of Him, for my requests are holy.

DAY 80

A fool utters all his mind:L but a wise man keeps it in till afterwards.

Proverbs 29: 11

Today, I will walk in the wisdom of God. I shall hold my tongue, and not speak all that is on my mind; many of my thoughts I shall keep secret.

Today, I shall be slow to give my opinion, and quick to pray about the matter at hand.

Today, I shall be careful not to offend anyone with my words. I shall ponder long before I speak.

DAY 81

The wicked flee when no man pursues: but the righteous are bold as a lion.

Proverbs 28: 1

Today, I will walk boldly in The Lord, and expect all of his promises to come forth in my life.

Today, I boldly believe a wonderful change is happening in my life.

Today, the wind of blessings shall blow into my life; blessings of finance, healings, peace, and joy.

DAY 82

Wait on the Lord: be of good courage, and he shall strengthen your heart: wait, I say, on the lord

Today, I will wait on The Lord; no matter what I am going through, or how long I have been going through, I am going to wait on God to send deliverance to me.

Today, I purpose to wait on God, for His help is on the way and will come in due time.

Today, I am joyful, for I know that God is on my side and is on the wait to help me; and though it might seem like He is tarrying, still, I will wait, for He is about to turn things around in my life.

DAY 83

And David was greatly distressed: for the people spoke of stoning him, because the soul of all the people was grieved, every man for his sons and for his daughters; but David encouraged himself in the lord his God.

1 Samuel 30; 6

Today, I will not wait for someone else to encourage me. Today, I will encourage myself in The Lord my God. Although my flesh might be weak and weakened, still, I shall encourage myself in my God, to fight on, to keep believing, to keep pressing my way forward.

Today, I am more than a conqueror; I have already won the battle. I walk in gladness and good tidings for my life. My enemies shall be defeated and I shall be exalted in The Lord.

Today, I say to myself, "Be encouraged, for God is not through with me yet." There is a purpose and a reason for what I am going through, but this too shall pass, and I will come forth like pure gold.

DAY 84

You are the salt of the earth; but if the salt have lost his savor, wherewith shall it be salted? It is thenceforth good for nothing, but to be cast out, and to be trodden under foot of men.

Matthew 5: 13

Today, I will display a good Christian attitude for others to follow. I shall season other's lives with my life.

Today, I will be a good example for others to follow. I will not forget that God has called me out to help others reach Him. My life shall put holy flavor in other's lives.

Today, I realize the depth of my salvation and what it should mean to others. I am the salt that God gave for others to depend upon.

DAY 85

You are the light of the world. A city that is set on an hill cannot be hid.

Matthew 5: 14

Today, I will the light of God that rests in my bosom shine forth in this dark world. I shall let my light shine in-spite of the turmoil in the streets. I shall let my light shine amidst the troubles of war and injustice all around me.

Today, I shall look pass my psychologically sick brothers around me, that's seeking to kill me and others like me, and let the light of God still shine forth from me.

Today, I will not allow fear to put my light out; I will not allow struggles to put my light out; no, today my light shall shine even brighter during these times of darkness.

Today, I shall let my light shine....Let it shine......let it shine.....let it shine.

DAY 86

For you are all the children of God by faith in Christ Jesus.

Galatians 3: 26

Today, I will walk in the fullness of my position in God through Christ Jesus. I am a son of God; The King's kid. I shall turn away anything and everything that denounce who I am, and only accept those things that confirm my position in God through Christ. I am of the royal seed; a son or daughter of God.

Today, I rejoice because of the power that God gave me in making me one of His children clothed in flesh.

Today, Satan is defeated, and his darkness is dispelled out of my life. The power of God rests on me, and today I will walk and talk and believe as a king's kid should. I am a child of The King.

DAY 87

The earth is the Lord's, and the fullness thereof; the world, and they that dwell therein.

Psalm 24: 1

Today, I give you praise oh Lord, for I know that everything that I can see, touch, and everything that is, belongs to you. I magnify The Lord this day, for He alone owns everything, and He has loaned me some of His properties to convenience me for the little while that I sojourn upon His earth.

Today, I thank Him for the many gifts that He has given unto me, and for allowing me a great degree of His comfort on His earth.

Today, I put all that mean me harm, in His hands, for they belongs to Him too; those that be over me on my job, that may sometimes treat me unfairly, I put them in His hands, for they belongs to him; they have to give account to Him for how they mistreat me, His child.

DAY 88

And the Lord shall make you plenteous in goods, in the fruit of your body, and in the fruit of your cattle, and in the fruit of your ground, in the land which the Lord sware unto your fathers to give you.

The Lord shall open unto you his good treasure, the heaven to give the rain unto your land in his season, and to bless all the work of yur hand: and you shall llend unto many nations, and you shall not borrow.

Deuteronomy 28: 11-12

Today, I am ready and willing to walk into the blessings that God has prepared for me. I take no account of where I work, or how much money I have right now, for my hope is in the Word of God and what He has promised me.

Today, I am financially blessed because He promised me financial security. Today is the beginning of me coming out of debt and walking in abundance.

Today, is the beginning of me becoming a lender and not a borrower. I am financially set in the Lord to lend to others. I will expect financial doors to become opened unto me.

Today, I shout in the Lord because He is blessing everything that I set out to do; He is ordering my steps into financial freedom, that I may be able to bless others.

Today, I am a lender and not a borrower. I am now walking out of debt and into plenty.

Today, I praise Him for the financial freedom that He has afforded me.

DAY 89

Where shall I go from your spirit? Or where shall I flee from your presence?

If I ascend up into heaven, you are there; if I make my bed in hell, behold, you are there.

Psalm 139: 7-8

Today, I thank you God, Heavenly Father, for always abiding with me. There is no place that I can go that you cannot get to me.

Today, I rejoice, for I am always in your presence. I praise you God, for always walking with me, and keeping me in your holy presence.

Today, when I leave home, you leave with me, and accompany me throughout my day, and when my load gets to heavy, and my burdens get too much for me to bear, you carry them for me, and even carry me when I am too weak to stand and journey on in that which you have destine for me.

Thank you Heavenly Father for not allowing me to leave your presence; and if I walk into some wayward situations or conditions today, remind me that I am not alone; you are here with me.

DAY 90

But now has he obtained a more excellent ministry, by how much also he is the mediator of a better covenant, which was established upon better promises.

Hebrews 8: 6

Today, I walk with no fear or envy, for I am in covenant with God, who made heaven and earth.

Today, I am in complete confidence, for God has established a covenant between Him and me; an everlasting covenant.

Today, I realize that because of the new covenant in Christ, God is my ally; I do not fight or walk alone. Today, He will assist me when I need assistance. His strength is my strength.

DAY 91

Beloved, I wish above all things that you may prosper
and be in health, even as your soul prospers.

3 John 1; 2

Today, I start my day praising God for prospering me and giving me good health, and renewed health. I thank Him for protecting me from sickness and disease.

Today, I magnify Him for saving my soul from a burning hell. Today I will laugh and worship him for wealth, health, strength of my body and soul.

DAY 92

A new commandment I give unto you, That you love one another as I have loved you, that you also love one another.

John 13: 34

Today, I will walk in the love of Christ. I will love my brothers in sisters regardless of their faults. I shall love as Christ has loved me.

Today, I will be quick to come to my brother's rescue, and have listening ears. I will love even when I don't understand; I will love any way.

DAY 93

For we wrestle not against flesh and blood, but against
principalities, against powers, against the rulers of the
darkness of this world, angainst spiritual wickedness in
high places.

Ephesians 6: 12

Today, I will remember who and what I am fighting against, and remind myself that I am fighting a spiritual fight with rulers of darkness.

Today, I shall pray mightily, realizing that prayer is my weapon and faith is my shield.

Today, I pray for my strength and my brothers and sisters in The Lord, that they be strong against the powers of darkness, and stand firm in the power of God.

DAY 94

Give me now wisdom and knowledge, that I may go out and come in before this people: for who can judge this your people, that is so great?

2 Chronicles 1: 10

Today, I will walk in the wisdom and knowledge of God. I will make sound decisions, and use the knowledge that I have acquire of God to dictate my steps today.

Today, I shall wait on The lord to give me deep holy decisions on matters that I shall come to face today, and wait on Him to bring the right knowledge that he has taught me up till now, that I might walk in the right direction.

Today, is a day of holy decision making, and righteous knowledge flowing from my mind to my lips, even down to my feet, that I might decide correctly to walk up the path of righteousness.

Today, I am a wised learned holy individual of God, that is decerning rightly in wisdom and knowledge.

DAY 95

Howbeit Jesus suffered him not, but says unto him, Go home to your friends, and tell them how great things the lord has done for you, and has had compassion on you.

Mark 5: 19

Today, I will be a vessel of praise unto my God, and show my friends and family how good and merciful He has been in my life.

Today, I will demonstrate how he saved me beyond my many faults and sins. I will tell them what God has done for me.

Today, I will tell my friends, loved ones, and everybody that I meet, of The lord's mercy and compassion upon all that will accept and believe on Him.

Today, I will make sure that my actions equal the words that I speak.

DAY 96

And they were all filled with the Holy Ghost, and began to speak with other tongues, as the Spirit gave them utterance.

Acts 2: 4

Today, I will let The Lord sit on my tongue, that the words that flow from my lips be ones that give Him praise, honor, and glory.

Today, I shall let the Holy Spirit use my mouth as a vessel of praise unto God. I will be careful of what I say, so that my lips will glorify Him in the presence of all that hear me.

Today, my words shall be holy and sanctified, that God might rest upon all of me.

Today, my lips shall speak of His goodness, mercy, and forgiveness.

DAY 97

Jesus answered and said unto him, Verily, verily, I say unto you, Except a man be born again, he cannot see the kingdom of God.

John 3: 3

Today, I am overjoyed that I have been born again by the blood of Jesus. He has made me fit for the Kingdom of God.

Today, I praise Him no matter what is going on in my life; I give God praise because He gave me the opportunity to be born again, and washed free of my sins through the blood of His only begotten son-Jesus the Christ.

Today, I glorify Him; I am happy because I have been born again.

Today, I shall tell others to be born again; all they have to do is accept Him as their Lord and savior, and make Him Lord of their lives, and they too, will be born again and fit for God's kingdom.

DAY 98

For thus says the Lord God of Israel, The barrel of meal shall not waste, neither shall the cruse of oil fail, until the day that the Lord send rain upon the earth.

1 kings 17: 14

Today, God has already supplied all of my needs; He will not allow me to walk in lack. He has already made a way for me. He has already opened some doors for me. I just need to turn around and open my eyes and see what The Lord has prepared for me.

Today, I will confess my abundance and expect God to fulfill His promises in my life. I have no need, for He will not let me run out of the things that I need. Help is always on the way.

Today, I am praising Him for filling my cupboards, my refrigerator, my car, my bank account, and my heart with love and holy expectancy.

DAY 99

As we have therefore opportunity, let us do good unto all men, especially unto them who are of the household of faith.

Galatians 6: 10

Today, I will seek an opportunity to bless someone else, especially those that are in Christ Jesus. I will plant seeds in others folk's lives.

Today, I shall seek out people to bless. I will bless with my money, with my mouth, and with my actions. I will lend a hand to those that are in need.

Today, I will seek to bless somebody, and not be in judgment; I shall leave the judging to God.

Today, Lord lead me to somebody that needs my help; somebody that I can bless that they might see you through my actions of giving.

DAY 100

And Elijah came unto all the people, and said, how long halt you between two opinions? If the Lord be God, follow him:; but if Baal, then follow him. And the people answered him not a word.

1 Kings 18: 21

Today, I have made up my mind to serve the Lord; to honor Him, and show all that I am a child of God. My opinion is firmly to The Lord.

Today, I will not be between two opinions. I will be a positive example of His power in my life.

Today, I decide to walk in power, and the majesty of the almighty God. I decide this day to serve Him and only Him. I release my old sinful ways and I decide this day to walk in the righteousness of God.

Today, I choose to live spiritually and physically. I will take good care of my body and mind. I choose to do those things that will bring health and wellness to my body and mind.

Today, I choose to eat right and exercise my body to health.

DAY 101

Give and it shall given unto you, good measure, pressed down, and shaken together, and running over, shall men give into your bosom. For with the same measure that you meet with it shall be measured to you again.

Luke 6: 38

Today, I shall began being a giver. I shall give to others in their times of need. I shall be slow to say no, and quick to lend assistance.

Today, I will walk in giving, knowing full well that my heavenly Father sees my giving, and rewards me accordingly. I realize today that I hinder my own blessings when I am stingy and refuse to be a giver. I cut off my blessing.

Today, I am giving to others because The lord will bless my family because of the fruit of my giving unto others.

Today, I know that whatever I give, God will always multiply my giving when He rewards me.

Today, I am a giver, and I receive the blessings because of my giving.

DAY 102

The Lord is a man of war: the Lord is his name.

Pharaoh's chariots and his host has he cast into the sea; his chosen captains also are drowned in the Red sea.

Exodus 15; 4

Today, I will not be overly concerned about my enemies or those that do not like me, for when they fight against me, they fight against The lord. He is my strong rock that fights with me and for me.

Today, I know that all they that go against me shall fail, for the lord is on my side. I will not be weary or afraid, for the battle is not mine; it is The Lord's.

Today, I will not be afraid, or walk in fear, for God walks with me. He will win my battles and defeat all of my enemies.

Today, I shall face my enemies and not be afraid. I shall pray for them, for they obviously do not realize who they are fighting-a child of the king, God's child.

DAY 103

You are of God, little children, and have overcome them: because greater is he that is in you, than he that is in the world.

1 John 4: 4

Today, I worship God for dwelling inside of me, and making me greater than the forces that be outside of me. He directs me from the inside out that I shall not fail.

Today, I will walk with my head uplifted regardless of what is going on in my life, for I know that sooner or later, I shall come forth in victory.

Today, I arise out of my bed feeling wonderfully made, and created in His image and after His likeness. I will rejoice and shout the victory over all that will come against me today.

Today, I release that greatness in me to come forth like a giant that has been asleep. I will conquer today. Those that I meet today that are down trodden, I shall try and lift their spirit and share with them the greatness inside of me.

Today, I confess that God is greater than anything that I shall confront this day, so today I shall walk in praise because of the greatness inside of me.

DAY 104

For the Lord of hosts has purposed, and who shall disannul it? And his hand is stretched out, and who shall turn it back?

Isaiah 14: 27

Today, I praise The Lord for stretching His mighty hand out before me and making my ways straight. Today, I will walk in the paths that He has made for me, paths to take me higher and raise me to a place of praise and thanksgiving.

Today, I will pay attention to note The Lord's hand in my path. Today, He shall usher in those people that shall assist me in becoming what He would have me to be. I thank Him for keeping His hands on me, and directing me.

Today, I will walk in His purpose, and remain under the umbrella of His hand.

DAY 105

Is anything too hard for the Lord? At the time appointed I will return unto you, according to the time of life, and Sarah shall have a son.

Today, I walk in joy and laughter, for I know that nothing that I shall come into today shall be too hard for my God. God is going to handle whatever troubles that might befall me, or whatever enemies that shall try to attack me.

Today, I rejoice, for there is nothing and nobody that is too hard for my God.

Today is going to be a good day; a day of new fresh beginnings for me; a day of blessings coming to me from The Lord.

Today, I expect to birth some of the miracles that God has placed in my bosom. Blessings that have evaded me and alluded me in the past, shall began to come forth for me today.

DAY 106

Not giving heed to Jewish fables, and commandments of men, that turn from the truth.

Titus 1: 14

Today, I will worship my God in truth. My mouth shall speak praises unto Him. His commandments shall be my guide.

Today, I shall turn away from the commandments of men, that dishonor my God.

Today, I lift my hands to worship Him, and show others the way to Him, and how to be thankful unto Him for all that He has done and is yet doing in our lives.

Today, I will rest upon God's truths.

DAY 107

I CAN DO ALL THINGS THROUGH Christ which strengthens me.

Philippians 4: 13

Today, failure is not an option for me. I will succeed at whatever I set my hands to do, for Christ is with me, and is giving me the strength to accomplish all of my tasks that will be put before me today.

Today, I start my day off with the thought that nothing is impossible for me, therefore, all things are possible.

Today, doors shall be opened unto me.

DAY 108

Bear you one another's burdens, and so fulfill the law of Christ.

Galatians 6: 2

Today, I will not be all about myself, but I shall try to help my fellow man with what he is trying to accomplish today. Those that have angered me and have treated me unjustly yesterday, I shall forgive today, and attempt to help them in any way that I can.

Today, I shall help my brother carry his cross, for I know that God helped me carry my cross.

Today, I start my day off extending my hand to those that are in need, to help them lessen their burdens.

DAY 109

And Jesus said unto the centurion, Go your way; and as you have believed, so be it done unto you. And his servant was healed in the selfsame hour.

Matthew 8: 13

Today, I will have a positive belief system. I believe that good things will come to me this day. I believe that God is going to send blessing to me this day. I believe that good finances, good health, good wealth, and good relationships shall began in my life this day.

Today, I believe that the sun of good fortune shall shine on me, and I will bath in the joy of The Lord.

Today, I believe and expect; I set the table for what I believe; right now in the name of Jesus the Christ, God's only begotten Son.

Today, I believe God's report for my life. I am healed, delivered, and set free from whatever has been binding me.

Today, I am believing for my family also, my children, my spouse, and my relatives and friends. Those that are connected to me shall be blessed.

DAY 110

Then was Jesus led up of the spirit into the wilderness to be tempted of the devil.

Matthew 4: 1

Today, I will resist any temptation that will come my way to cause me to deviate from my anointing and my divine purpose. I will successfully resist the ploys of the devil.

Today, I will defeat the tempter when he comes at me. I already know that he is coming, so right now, I prepare myself through prayer.

Today, I will bring my flesh under control by the power of God. I will resist.

Today, I am stronger; I am better; I am an over comer, for today, I will defeat the tempter.

DAY 111

Prove your servants, I beseech you, ten days; and let them give us pulse to eat, and water to drink.

Daniel 1: 12

Today, I will take control of my will. I will not allow myself to be overpowered or overcome by food or any other weakness that I have had in times pass. I am in control of my body. I will not be ruled by food.

Today is the beginning of me eating right, and putting nutritiously good food into my mouth. I will not be defeated by my fork or spoon.

Today, I begin eating those things that will foster good health in my life; foods that will keep my blood pressure right, my blood sugar right, and all of my other bodily measurements.

Today, I am in control; I will eat right and exercise, that I might live a long and fruitful life in The Lord.

DAY 112

And the Lord God said, It is not good that the man should be alone; I will make him an help meet for him.

Genesis 2: 18

Today, I will take responsibility for my relationships; I will not blame others. I am responsible for the relationship between me and my mate. I shall begin to be the best that I can be in this relationship, and not be dependent upon how they treat me or react to me.

Today, I am the best person that I can be, and I will build the best relationship that I can build. I will forget about the hurt of the past, and the let downs and failures of my mate, or the other party in my relationships. I will work to bring happiness and joy into this relationship.

Today, I will begin to journey ahead in this relationship expecting the best because I will give my best.

DAY 113

And he shall be like a tree planted by the rivers of water, that brings forth his fruit in his season; his leaf also shall not wither; and whatsoever he does shall prosper.

Psalms 1: 3

Today, I will walk into my blessings, for it is my season. I have waited; I have prayed, and now I am expecting today to be blessed abundantly of The Lord.

Today, I shall flourish like a tree by a river of water. I will blossom and help others to be blessed.

Today, I began walking in prosperity; I am going to prosper at whatever I set my hands to do because God has already blessed my way.

Today, the fruits of my labor shall come forth; the fruits that I have been waiting for will meet me today. I am blessed and prosperous.

DAY 114

Fret not yourself because of evildoers, neither be you envious against the workers of iniquity.

Psalm 37: 1

Today, I will not fear those that are evil workers. I will walk in the security and under the protective hand of God. I shall not be afraid of those that are seeking to kill the innocent for their own causes. God is my avenger. He will not fail. He will not fret because of the evil workers.

Today, I will walk in no fear. God will soon bring His wrath upon them for shedding the blood of the innocent. God is my strong tower; He will keep the city.

Today, I will not be worried or fearful, for my God is still in control; He will soon cut off the evil workers.

DAY 115

And I will give unto you the keys of the kingdom of heaven: and what so ever you shall bi8nd on earth shall be bound in heaven: and what so ever you shall loose on earth shall be loosed in heaven.

Matthew 16: 19

Today, I bind those things that have been holding me back, and I lose the spirit of courage upon me right now.

Today, I bind that spirit of poverty and sickness from my life, and I lose the spirit of wealth and health. I will no longer live in want and sickness, but I profess healing and plenty in my life right now. Everything that the devil stole from me shall be returned right now-in abundance.

Today, I use the keys of prayer to bind the spirit of confusion and adversity from my life, and I lose the spirit of peace and harmony right now.

Today, I shall use all the keys from heaven that Jesus gave me to set me free and bring abundance in my life.

Today, I lose the power of God in my life and my family's life. I am set free by the power of Jehovah.

DAY 116

Let all your things be done with love.

1 Corinthians 16: 14

Today, I am walking in love; I will love my enemies as well as my friends. Because of love, I will be quick to forgive and ready to give assistance.

Today, I am filled with the love of God, so I will look beyond other's faults and mistakes. I am filled with the love of God.

Today, the Holy Spirit covers me because I walk in love.

Today, everything that I do shall be moved by love. I love all of God's creation.

DAY 117

Against an elder receive not an accusation, but before two or three witnesses.

1 Timothy 5: 19

Today, I will walk in obedience, and honor those that are over me. I will respect those that are in authority, for I realize that God has put them in a higher position over me. I respect and honor my leaders.

Today, I realize that to the degree that I honor and respect those that God has place in authority over me, is the same degree that I honor and respect The Lord.

Today, I pray for my leaders, and assist them in whatever way that I can. I will be a good follower, knowing that this shall enable me to be a good leader some day.

Today, I pray for all that are in authority; my father, my mother, my pastor, my spouse; I pray for all authority.

DAY 118

Are they not all ministering spirits, sent forth to minister
for them who shall be heirs of salvation.

Hebrews 1: 14

Today, I rejoice and praise God, for He has not left me alone. He has given me angels to assist me during my daily walk with Him.

Today, a company of angels shall defeat the devils attack against me. The angels shall make my way straight.

Today, I praise The Lord, for I walk not alone. The angels of salvation walk with me, and fight with and for me.

Today, I worship God for the company of angels that He has given to help me. I am not defeated. I will overcome today.

DAY 119

Let not your heart be troubled: you believe in God, believe also in me.

John 14: 1

Today, I shall not allow myself to worry about anything, for Jesus has given me the victory. I shall not waist my time worrying about things that is beyond my control, or things that I cannot change. God gave me the victory on earth and Jesus went away to prepare a place in heaven for me.

Today, I praise Him. I believe that Jesus has already given me the victory; anything that comes against me shall be defeated.

Today, I believe in the power of God, that He is able to keep me in all of my way.

Today, I worship Him for preparing a place for me in heaven.

Today, I will not be sorrowful, or sad, or distressed, or worried, for I have the victory through Christ Jesus my Lord.

Today, I've will defeat whatever the devil sends my way. Hallelujah, praise be unto Him for giving me the victory.

DAY 120

And God said, Let us make man in our image, after our likeness: and let them have dominion over the fish of the sea, and over the fowl of the air, and over the cattle, and over all the earth, and over every creeping thing that creeps upon the earth.

Genesis 2: 26

Today, I give God thanks for making me in His image and His likeness. I cannot be defeated or destroyed, for I am made after Him, and I contain the power and greatness of Him.

Today, I rejoice, for I am God's representative; I walk in His power and might.

Today, I live in thanksgiving, for I am in the very image and likeness of God. On this earth, I am of the royal blood and linage of Christ.

Today, I realize that I am the personage of God upon earth. I walk in His power and His presence amongst men. I praise Him today and rejoice. I am God's child in the flesh.

NOTES

NOTES

NOTES

NOTES

NOTES

NOTES

NOTES

NOTES

Printed in the United States
By Bookmasters